BY - HARISH ARORA
(MARKETING & BUSINESS COACH)

JAI GURUDEV!
JAI SHREE GANESHAY NAMAH!!!

COURSE - 1

• THREE •
DAYS COURSE

PRICE
₹ 9000/-
FREE

T&C APPLY

• INDEX •

CONCEPT OF THE AFFILIATE MARKETING –

- **Actually what is Affiliate Marketing?**

- **Advantages of Affiliate Marketing?**

- **Disadvantages of Affiliate Marketing?**

- **Who can Do Affiliate Marketing?**

- **What is the right time to do Start Affiliate Marketing?**

- **How Affiliate Marketing works?**

- **Affiliate Marketing Success Rule?**

- **8 Steps of Affiliate Marketing Guide**

" THE BEST PREPARATION FOR TOMORROW IS DOING YOUR BEST TODAY "

— H. Jackson brown, jr.

MORE LINKS :

+91 97111 09725

WWW.FACEBOOK.COM/MARKETINGHARISH

WWW.INSTAGRAM.COM/MARKETINGHARISH

T&C APPLY

DAY - 1.

ACTUALLY WHAT IS AFFILIATE MARKETING?

▶ It is a technique of selling the products online.

▶ In which the owner of the product/s allows someone for increasing his sale by targeting the audience and that affiliate gets the commission over the product.

▶ Affiliate Marketing is a profitable business in which the affiliate does not need to create his/her own product.

▶ The affiliate increases the sale by using the Social Media Platforms, Blogging or Creating through own websites. Affiliate Marketing products a good source of Income.

You must have to know that the CONCEPT OF AFFILIATE MARKETING existed before the Web, but its GREW on the web due to Online Shopping & Digital Goods Market.

In 1989, Mr. William J. Tobin setup the First Affiliate Marketing Program for his Company PC Flowers & Gifts.

T&C APPLY

MARKETING HARISH

ADVANTAGES OF THE AFFILIATE MARKETING?

NOW WE WILL SEE VARIOUS ADVANTAGES AND DISADVANTAGES OF AFFILIATE MARKETING.

S. N.	MIN. INVESTMENT	MAX. RETURNS
01	Social Media Platforms	Shared commission by advertisers/ owners are
02	Blog/ Websites/ Hosting	pretty high upto 90%
03	Learn to Skills SEO=>Youtube Video=>Web Designing	
04	No Shop/ Space requirement	
05	No need to buy products like distributor/shopkeeper	
06	You only need to focus on your skills to earn through Affiliate Marketing	

T&C APPLY

2. If we see from the company point of view they have to pay to Affiliate only for the results they give. The company gets a free ad space.

3. If we see from the Affiliate point of view they have to just provide ad space for the promotion of merchant's, products and services and hence they have a good income with the end of the day.

4. Advertisement of a product in a huge audience provides exposure and recognition for every brand.

5. Affiliate consumers that are bought by Affiliate help to get the important information about the recent trends or demands in the market.

MARKETING HARISH

BY - HARISH ARORA
(MARKETING & BUSINESS COACH)

WWW.MARKETINGHARISH.COM

DISADVANTAGES OF THE AFFILIATE MARKETING?

1. Suppose any Affiliate performs the false advertisement then it will affect the reputation of merchant's. And nowadays there is various Affiliate engage in this scheme.

2. If any merchant is having several Affiliate then he may have to bear a high commission cost.

3. If we see from an Affiliate point of view, there is a risk on his head if the merchant twisted and shut down the programs without paying to Affiliate he can't do anything.

4. Sometimes Affiliate is charged with membership charge and the program shows of providing a high commission to the Affiliate. But in natural the merchant tricks and pays very less from the promised amount.

MARKETING HARISH

5. There is the various unscrupulous individual who hi Jack the commission from the middle in the process of Affiliate linking.

No doubt there are various disadvantages of Affiliate Marketing but still, it is one of the good sources of income. For avoiding this risk marketer have to be very smart and perform some homework and research. They have to take some security measures for negotiating with the disadvantages of Affiliate Marketing and enjoy the advantages of Affiliate Marketing.

MARKETING HARISH

WHO CAN DO AFFILIATE MARKETING?

FOREVER READY TO LEARN - You should pass the craving to learn, with the ability to be prepared. Whenever you start, you need to utilize the experience from others to learn more while you go.
You should need to trust your MENTOR.

TIME and EFFORTS - You should be prepared to invest time and work to assist your business with developing, regardless of whether you see no prompt outcomes. You need to persistence more with the right system.

Determination - The third quality you want is DETERMINATION. To get success in the affiliate marketing world, you should always PUSH YOURSELF forward.

DISCIPLINE - The fourth quality is self-discipline. If you teach yourself to work with you everyday Heart and Soul, you will be so much closer to achieving your goals and making your dreams come true.

Good faith and FOCUS - The last yet not the most un-quality you want to have is Optimism. Terrible mentalities ought to never deter an offshoot advertiser from the quest for her fantasies to make life.

WHAT IS THE RIGHT TIME TO START AFFILIATE MARKETING?

The right time to start Affiliate Marketing is TODAY & NOW.

Affiliate Marketing now on BORN PHASE and its a HIGHLY GROWING INDUSTRY. A lot of merchants/ product owners choosing Affiliate Market/ Network than Invest on Ads now. So, opportunities are waiting, you please start with hope & positive attitude.

T&C APPLY

MARKETING HARISH

HOW AFFILIATE MARKETING WORKS?

Before discuss How Affiliate Marketing Works, I want to clear Myths about Affiliate Marketing?

Affiliate Marketing is not a Quick Rich Scheme.

You don't need to Influence in English and you don't need to have any technical skill.

Affiliate Marketing is not a SCAM

To do affiliate marketing, you have to know, how operate Smartphone. Just knowledge to emails, Social Media Marketing etc. etc.

Let's know now
"HOW AFFILIATE MARKETING WORKS"?

The company or organization that wants to promote its products, it offers its Affiliate Program. Now any other person like a blog or website owner joins that program, then the company or organization gives him any banner or link etc. to promote their products on his blog or website. Now in the next step, that person puts that link or banner on his blog or website in different ways. Now many visitors come to that person's blog or website. When a visitor clicks on that link or banner and reaches the website of the company or organization offering the affiliate program and buys something or signs up for a service, then that company or organization commissions him in return.

T&C APPLY

MARKETING HARISH

AFFILIATE MARKETING SUCCESS RULE?

For further success, first of all you have to know what work you have done in the past and got any benefit from them or not and if you got it then how did you get it and if there was loss then why was it done. You can improve many things from which the growth of your Affiliate Marketing will start.

HAVE COMPLETE INFORMATION ABOUT THE PRODUCT-

Whatever you do Affiliate Marketing, try to have complete knowledge about that product, because when you have a good knowledge about a product, only then you will be able to tell about it well and give advice to others.

But if you do not have information about the product and you will tell others that it is good and you should buy them, then you will not see the things of the expert, from which users will feel that they did not get good information and they will not buy the product from your Affiliate Link, that's why Know about the product well and tell your users in such a way whether they should buy or not.

If once the buyer understands your explanation and he wants to buy, then at the same time he will buy by clicking on your Affiliate Link and you will easily get Affiliate Commission.

Engage Users -

Most successful Affiliate Marketers talk to their visitors. If you have a blog, allow comments. This will give you a chance to connect with your visitors.

Yes, you will need to do some hard work to filter Spam Comment, but if you answer most of your comments and keep talking to the visitors to your website, then they will come back to your website to know the answer to their question. Which will increase traffic on your site.

The more people connect to your website, they will come to your website again and again, which will increase the traffic of your website and also the conversion.

Focus on providing information rather than selling -

You should think about helping your visitors and providing them with useful information so that they keep coming back. If you look at sites that rank well on multiple keywords in your niche and get conversions, you will find that such websites mostly focus on providing useful information to their users.

See your competitor, what they are doing that is increasing their Affiliate Sales and analyze about those things.

Always analyze and improve and update -

You should always try to improve and update your analysis and content. This is the easiest way to get success in any thing, it is to analyze what he has already done, then you should also do Competitor Analysis and see how your Competitor writes articles and what is the process. Is . And you should keep updating your content from time to time so that it is beneficial for SEO and can rank your website.

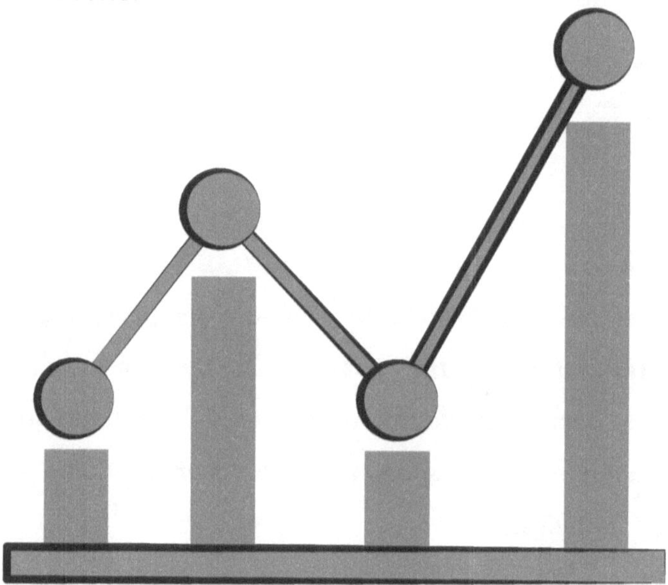

8 STEPS OF AFFILIATE MARKETING GUIDE?

The 8 steps of Affiliate Marketing guide.

Step 1. Website/ Blog Creation -

Creation of website "For beginning the affiliate marketing concept the very best market is online website and for creating a website set up the best way is to use WordPress.

Step 2. Selection of the topic.

This is one of the most important steps the topic you are selecting must be interested and you must have an interest in it. Your interest will help you to add the best content on your website.

Step 3. Creating content for your website.

There must be a continuous process for adding content on your website for this process again you can use a web platform such as WordPress. The content you upload must be original (plagiarism-free) and of high quality. Also, you must check the content provided by you must be helpful and interesting. This will help you to run your website successfully.

Step 4. - **Searching for the offers that match your content.**

Famous affiliate companies are Amazon, Google, LinkShare

T&C APPLY

Step 5. Addition OF THE ADVERTISEMENT AND THE LINKS

In this step, you have to add the links or ads to the website created by you. If WordPress is used for this purpose then we get the advantage of adding the websites at the sidebar or individual post.

Step 6. Step up a clear call to your action for traffic.

As the public start to visit your website your earning begins. As the people buy goods your commission is credited. Sometimes even if they sign-up for your website the commission is on your hand.

Step 7. Time for affiliates payment

No matter what affiliate you are using for the website. Just the thing you have to take care is the terms of network you are working on. Every network has its payout method, thresholds, and requirements. Reporting system of each site is also different. Each report specifies how much you have earned by the three factors value for each visit (pay-per-click), registration (pay-per-lead), or every purchaser (pay-per-sale).

Step 8. Repeat the same procedure and be successful!

Once you made your website successful for the website you will just print the cash. You can make the number of affiliate sites on the number of topics. Learn from the mistakes and your strong points from your first site and work accordingly in the second one. In this way, you can double your payment every time.

T&C APPLY

BY - HARISH ARORA
(MARKETING & BUSINESS COACH)

WWW.MARKETINGHARISH.COM

TASK 1

Answer the Questions –

1. What is your Goal in Life?

2. What is the eligibility to do Affiliate Marketing?

3. What is the role of an Affiliate in Affiliate Marketing?

TASK 2

Create a Video to describe How Affiliate Marketing Works and Upload the same on your any of Social Media Platform with Hashtag #marketingharish .

MORE LINKS :

+91 97111 09725

WWW.FACEBOOK.COM/MARKETINGHARISH

WWW.INSTAGRAM.COM/MARKETINGHARISH

T&C APPLY

BY - HARISH ARORA
(MARKETING & BUSINESS COACH)

WWW.MARKETINGHARISH.COM

DAY - 2.

TACTICS AFFILIATE MARKETING

▶ **Types of Affiliate Marketing?**

▶ **Affiliate Networks?**

▶ **Tools used to Start Affiliate Marketing?**

▶ **Why a website is Important in Affiliate Marketing?**

▶ **Modules in Affiliate Marketing?**

I WOULD PREFER A SWORD TO FIGHT

DUEL, BUT A PEN TO PLAN A WAR.

— ROBERT THIER,

MORE LINKS :

+91 97111 09725

WWW.FACEBOOK.COM/MARKETINGHARISH

WWW.INSTAGRAM.COM/MARKETINGHARISH

T&C APPLY

TYPES OF AFFILIATE MARKETING?

There are many types of affiliate marketing, it has 3 main types:

Unattached Affiliate Marketing

In this way, affiliates also publish those products and services on their site, about whose they do not know much. For example, if there is a blog of an Affiliate, who is in fashion and designer clothes and on that blog he publishes the ad of any courier company, then it is called Unattached Affiliate Marketing.

Related Affiliate Marketing

In this way, in Affiliate marketing, Affiliates publish or post those ads on their blog or website, which are related to blogs or websites.

Involved Affiliate Marketing

In this way, in Affiliate marketing, Affiliates are marketing those products or services in their blogs, which they used themselves.
In this way, ads or banners are not put up in Affiliate marketing, but affiliates can make their own blogs.

I mention and recommend them in the curriculum. For example, if an Affiliate has any the designer appreciates the clothes that he used for making the clothes, so it's kind of Involved Affiliate marketing will be called.

T&C APPLY

TYPES OF AFFILIATE PRODUCTS?

- **PPC (Pay Per Click Model)**
- **PPL (Pay Per Lead)**
- **PPS (Pay Per Sale)**
- **CPA (Cost Per Action)**
- **One Time Commissions**
- **Recurring Commissions**

• PPC (Pay Per Click Model) :

In this type of affiliate marketing, whatever link is provided to the affiliate marketer, every click on it is paid according to it and this is what we call pay per click affiliate marketing.

Pay per click type of affiliate marketing is run by the advertisers, in this, whatever ad is run on our platform, we get that advertising program according to the number of clicks on it.

This model is quite easy and in this if our site generates good traffic, then we will get more clicks on the ads running on our site, which will increase our earning money growth.

SOME PAY PER CLICK AFFILIATE MARKETING EXPLAINS -

media.net - It comes second after Google Adsense. This is also a very good advertising platform. We can earn a lot by working with it. But media.net only gives approval to English bloggers.

Ezoic - This is also an advertising company, in this program also we generate very good revenue by running the ad and clicking it. And this is a google adsense certified program.

• PPL (Pay Per Lead) Model Affiliate Marketing -

As the name suggests, in this affiliate marketing model, marketers earn commission by generating leads. That's why this type of model is called PPL (Pay Per Lead) Affiliate Marketing Model.

In the PPL model, affiliate marketers get visitors to sign-up, opt-in, fill up the form, use the visitor's contact number with permission.

Pay Per Lead Marketing is a fine tuned marketing in which the lead generated is a valuable lead in which the chances of converting to sale are maximum.

The commission generated in this is done under this fine-tuned lead generation program.

Because the conversion rate is very high in this.

T&C APPLY

MARKETING HARISH

Some PPL Model Affiliate Marketing Programs -

LinkedIn Learning Affiliate Marketing Program -

The LinkedIn Learning Program helps those people who want to learn business, tech or some new creative skills. In this, there are experts associated with these courses, who teach us all this. Now they also have an affiliate program in which any marketer can earn commission by generating valuable leads.

Skillshare Affiliate Marketing Program -

Skillshare is an online learning group where free and paid courses related to different fields are available. That's why we can commission for this program also by generating valuable leads.

• Pay Per Sale (PPS) Model Affiliate Marketing -

This is the real model of affiliate marketing or it is called affiliate marketing. Whenever we sell any product or any services of a business partner by doing affiliate marketing, we get commission in return for that.

Many affiliate marketers use this type of marketing and get good commission. some examples of this -

- • amazon associates
- • share a sale
- • commission junction

There are three types of commission received in this model -

1. SideWide Commission -

Sidewide Commission we get as a complementary, like by selling some package of a travel company, we get a chance to go to some place for free. Or we get a product from someone's side. This is a sidewide commission in a way.

2. One Time Commission -

In the affiliate model with one time commission, we get commission only once on selling any product or services, this is called one time commission. Most similar programs are available in affiliate marketing.

In this, we sell any product and we get whatever commission is on it.

3. Recurring Commissions Model -

This commission model is a very good affiliate marketing model, in which we get commission on whatever product or services we sell at the same time as well as when the customer gets that service or product updated. Yes, we keep getting commission on that too.

Such models are basically seen more in the software industry, insurance market, where whenever we update any software or policy, we still get its commission.

T&C APPLY

- **Pillars in Affiliate Marketing?**

Affiliate Marketing based on the 3 Pillars, which are

1. Product Owner/ The Marchant –
- Also can say Creater/ Seller/ Brand/ Vendor

2. The Customer –
- Can say Consumer/ Buyer the Products

3. The Affiliate –
- also called Publisher/ Individuals/ Companies

- **Affiliate Marketing Definitions -**
There are some rules or definitions used in Affiliate

Marketing, about them should know, who is an affiliate -

1. AFFILIATES:

Affiliates are called those who join an affiliate program and promote their

products on their sources such as blog or website.

2. AFFILIATE MARKETER -

Affiliate Marketer is called those who join the Affiliate Program of a company

and sell their products themselves or through Blog, Website.

MARKETING **HARISH**

3. AFFILIATE MARKETPLACE - There are many such companies which run different affiliate programs, there are many types of affiliate programs, they are called market places.

4. AFFILIATE ID- This is a new id which is obtained by Signup, each is given a unique id in the Affiliate Program, which helps in collecting information at the time of sale.

5. AFFILIATE LINK - There is a link to any product that you promote and sell, with the help of these links the visitor goes to the website and the affiliate company gets to know through whom the visitor has come to the website and the product On buying, you get commission.

6. PAYMENT MODE - The medium through which payment of commission is given to Affiliates is called Payment Mode. There are various modes of payment like check, wire transfer, paypal, direct transfer to Bank Accounts etc.

7. COMMISSION: The amount, which is given to the affiliate according to each sale. This can be a percentage of the sale or a pre-determined amount.

8. LINK CLOCKING: The link of affiliate program gets bigger and if you put that big link on the blog or anywhere, then people will get the spam link and then there will be no sale, that's why there is only one solution i.e. link cloaking means link shorten.

9. AFFILIATE MANAGER: Some people are appointed by some Affiliate programs to help Affiliates and to give them tips, they are called Affiliate Managers.

10. PAYMENT THRESHOLD - The minimum amount that when you earn, you will be paid your dues. The payment threshold amount of different programs is different.

T&C APPLY

- ## What are Affiliate Networks?

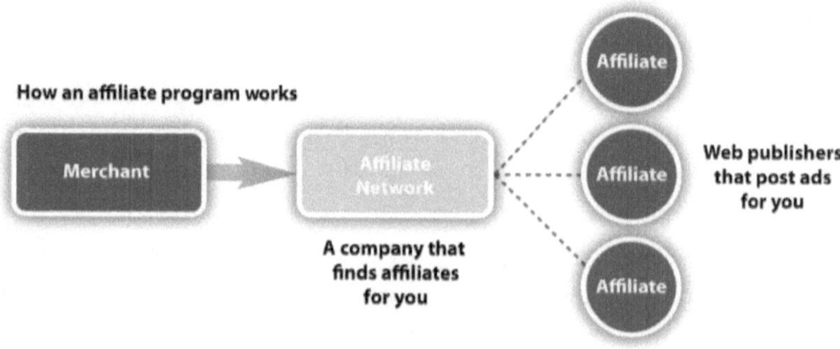

It is a third party/ Intermediately between advertisers and affiliate.

It gives instant access to thousands of advertisers from different niche.

Manages advertisers relationship and lookout for your payment every month.

Track each and every sales made by you.

Great support and management skills to help you out.

Ex. AFFILIATE NETWORKS -

Clickbank	– Digital Products
Market Health	- Health Products
Commission Junction	-
Share A Sale	-
Upclick	- Software/ Digital Products
Amazon Associates	- Physical Products
Many more	

(will discuss tomorrow on how to generate high income by these networks)

• Tools used to Start Affiliate Marketing?

- Niche Websites (Domain+Hosting+WordPress)
- Mobile Apps
- Blogging
- Youtube Channel
- FB Page
- Email Marketing
- Social Media Marketing (FB/Linkdin/Twitter/SEO/Quora)

T&C APPLY

MARKETING HARISH

Why a website is Important in Affiliate Marketing?

- **You can do affiliate marketing without website and using any one or more Social Media Platforms, but I strongly recommend that a Commercial Website/ Landing Pages will give you better conversion.**

- **IF YOU ARE USING FREE TRAFFIC SOURCE – website is must**

- **IF YOU ARE USING PAID TRAFFIC – than you can skip website.**

T&C APPLY

MARKETING HARISH

TASK 1

Answer the Questions –

1. How many types of Affiliate Products?
2. What is the Importance of Link Cloacking Affiliate Marketing?
3. Which kind of Tools needed in Affiliate Marketing?
4. What you understand about Affiliate Networks?

TASK 2

Create an Account on Instagram/ FB. Make Reels to show Affiliate Definitions and Upload on your Instagram/FB Account with #marketingharish.

TASK 3

Make a Video to describe the Value of Niche in Affiliate Marketing and Upload the same on your any of Social Media Platform with Hashtag #marketingharish.

BY - HARISH ARORA
(MARKETING & BUSINESS COACH)

WWW.MARKETINGHARISH.COM

DAY - 3.

IMPLIMENTATION –

▶ **Niche Finding**

▶ **Affiliate Marketing Success Mantra**

▶ **Affiliate Marketing Implementation Strategy**

▶ **Lead Magnet**

▶ **Landing Page**

▶ **Traffic Source – Free & Paid**

▶ **Affiliate Network**

▶ **Task Day – 3**

MORE LINKS :

📞 +91 97111 09725

📘 WWW.FACEBOOK.COM/MARKETINGHARISH

📷 WWW.INSTAGRAM.COM/MARKETINGHARISH

T&C APPLY

• Niche Finding –

Niche is very IMPORTANT in Affiliate Marketing. If you have not a clear niche, you can not grow on Affiliate Marketing.

Let me explain, How to find Niche for Affiliate Marketing ?

First of all, you should choose any 5 category for niche, according to you, like

1. Health

2. Technology

3. Money

4. Insurance

5. Movies

6. Relationship

After that the category which you have selected, Try to create content/ posts in all of them. After writing 3-4 posts in each category, you will come to know that you like to write on which topic/category. By doing this you will find the category of your choice. Which is a big deal to find out your interest.

After posts on Social Media platform in each category, you will come to know that you are getting traffic by writing on which post. The post on which you get more traffic, more views & more likes, that is your niche. In this way you can choose your niche.

Otherwise you can choose your niche according to your hobby.

T&C APPLY

- ## Affiliate Marketing Success Mantra?

    - **ADD VALUE BEFORE SELL ANYTHING**

    - **Must have PATIENCE**

    - **FAITH on YOURSELF**

    - **STRATEGY**

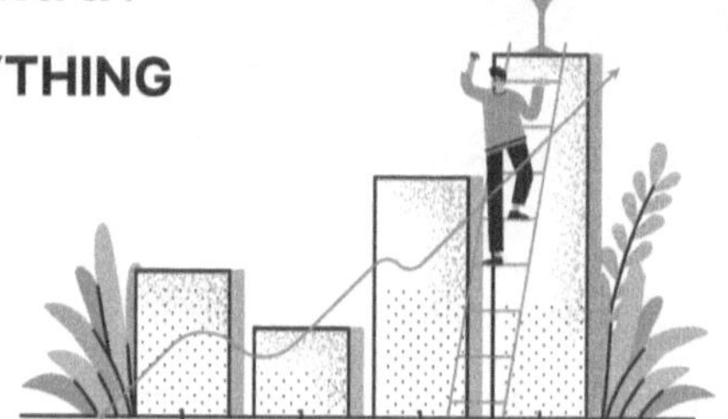

- ## Affiliate Marketing Implementation Strategy?

To get success in Affiliate Marketing, you must have a Strategy to implement.
First of all you have to choose a Right Product (according to your niche).

Right Product ➡ Hobby/ Health/ Wealth/ Interest must & comfortable in
Choose

Information ➡ After choosing the right product (according to your niche),
you have to collect complete information about your product
before promote it.

Keyword ➡ Find atleast 10-15 keywords to promote your product

- ## How to convert Lead into Sales?

RIGHT PRODUCT ➡ LEAD MAGNET (Give your full energy) ➡ WEBSITE/
LANDING PAGE ➡ Email Marketing ➡ Free Traffic/Paid Traffic ➡ SALES

T&C APPLY

MARKETING HARISH

• LEAD MAGNET ?

A lead-magnet is, in simple words, a free offer of a service or product that gives an idea of your company that is capable of solving a customer's problem. In marketing, a lead-magnet is an "advantage" that allows a potential customer to solve their own problem and get to know your company. No sales funnel can exist without it.

• The task that the lead-magnet solves is:

- Presenting the product to the audience.
- Positioning your uniqueness.
- Gaining an advantage over the competitor.
- Expanding customer base.
- Improving product credibility and increasing sales.

• Characteristics of a good lead-magnet:

- Useful: Solves buyer's problem.
- Simple and clear from name to content and design.
- Specific: Does not cover multiple topics at once.
- Unique: It does not copy existing lead-magnets.
- Valuable: This is not explicit data from Google-search links, the information included reflects your expertise.
- Available: This can be downloaded or opened in a matter of seconds.

T&C APPLY

- **Types of lead-magnets:**

1. Educational lead-magnet :

- A chapter of a book or the book itself (usually in an electronic version).
- REPORT OR RESEARCH: "Market Player Movement Report for the First Quarter of 2011."
- FORECAST: "Estimated Changes in the Educational Projects Market." Invitation to a private professional chat in Telegram, Facebook, Slack.
- EMAIL COURSE: "Write your first Telegram bot in 15 characters."
- Recordings of webinars, lectures or events.

2. Entertainment Lead-Magnets :

- Test results: "Pass the quiz and find out which soft skills you need to upgrade right now."
- Results of the game: "Find out what awaits you in the New Year by choosing a card."
- Selection of entertainment content (only your website should be used. Avoid using third party resources).

3. Lead-magnets that drive people to buy :

(they are at the bottom of the sales funnel, not at the beginning)

- Discount on first purchase, bonus for purchase, or any promotion.
- Demo of your product (it should be free, even if it doesn't cost above several tens of bucks).
- Free consultation from experts (according to your product).

T&C APPLY

MARKETING HARISH

• Landing Page?

The page on which more users visit is called landing page. If we explain it in easy language, then if you have a website, then the home page of that website is a kind of Landing Page.

Actually Landing page is a short form of website. A website is made up of many web pages, but the landing page is made up of only one page.

The landing page is great for affiliate marketing. The conversion rate on the landing page is quite good.

Advantages of Landing Page –

I hope you know what is a Landing Page? Let us now know what are the benefits of creating a landing page?

It is very short in comparison to the landing page of the website. We can optimize the landing page very well.

Landing page is very best for affiliate marketing. With the help of this we can target, the target audiences, which increases the conversion. And our sales start getting very good.

T&C APPLY

If you share any affiliate link on social media many times. Then your link gets blocked and you can put all your affiliate links on the landing page. This does not pose any threat to you and your website.

You can also create a landing page for free and paid.

How to Create Landing Page for free?

Now let's talk about how you can create a landing page. Friends, there are many such platforms where you have to pay money to make a landing page.

But today I will tell you the names of some such platforms where you can create a landing page for free.

Landing Page Platform - Free

Freshworks.com

LinkTr.ee (Blocked On Pinterest)

And Many more

Creating a landing page is very easy.

Let me show you a landing page on Linktr.ee

T&C APPLY

BY - HARISH ARORA
(MARKETING & BUSINESS COACH)

WWW.MARKETINGHARISH.COM

1ST STEP ➡ First of all, search linktree in any of your browsers. After this click on the first result linktr.ee

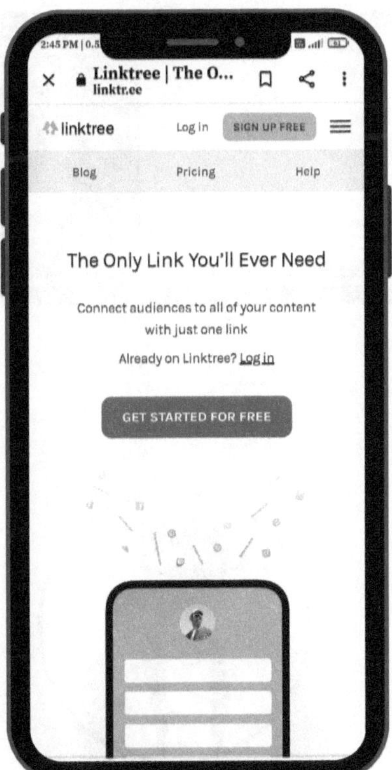

BY - HARISH ARORA
(MARKETING & BUSINESS COACH)

T&C APPLY

MORE LINKS :

📱 **+91 97111 09725**

📘 **WWW.FACEBOOK.COM/MARKETINGHARISH**

📷 **WWW.INSTAGRAM.COM/MARKETINGHARISH**

BY - HARISH ARORA
(MARKETING & BUSINESS COACH)

WWW.MARKETINGHARISH.COM

2ND STEP ➡ After this you have to create an account by clicking on get started free. Give your username carefully. Your username will be mentioned in the link of this landing page.

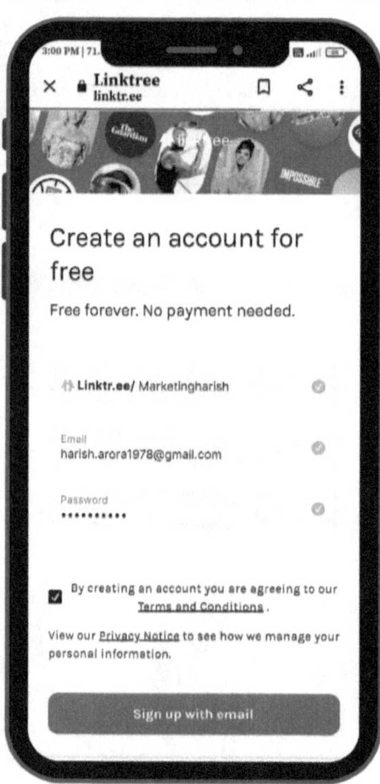

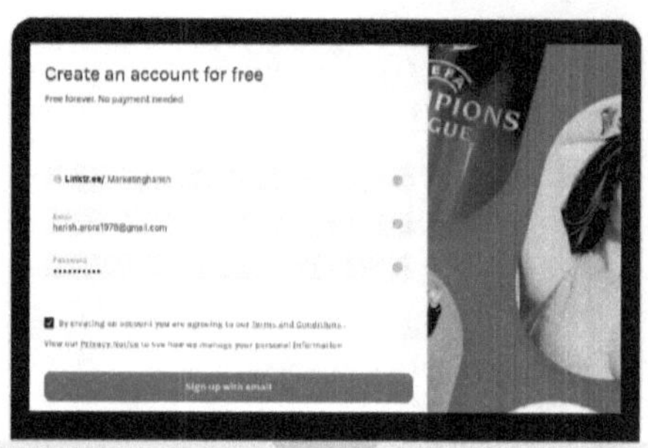

BY - HARISH ARORA
(MARKETING & BUSINESS COACH)

MORE LINKS :

+91 97111 09725

WWW.FACEBOOK.COM/MARKETINGHARISH

WWW.INSTAGRAM.COM/MARKETINGHARISH

T&C APPLY

WWW.MARKETINGHARISH.COM

3rd Step ➡ A verification link will be sent to your email id. You have to verify. After this you will be login to the dashboard.

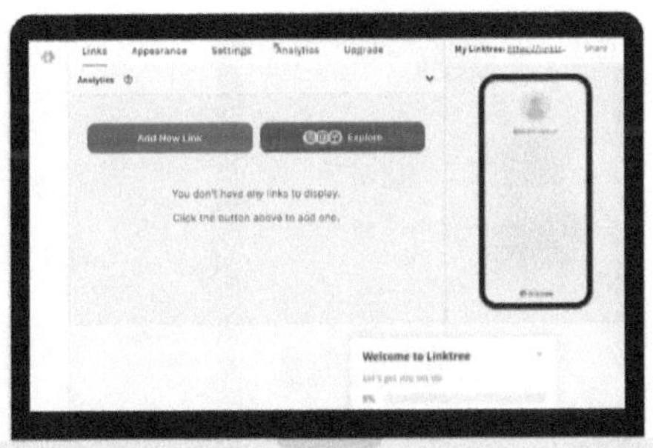

BY - HARISH ARORA
(MARKETING & BUSINESS COACH)

MORE LINKS :

+91 97111 09725

WWW.FACEBOOK.COM/MARKETINGHARISH

WWW.INSTAGRAM.COM/MARKETINGHARISH

T&C APPLY

4th Step (You will see an option of add new link in the dashboard. Click on that option and fill in the title and url of the products you want to promote.

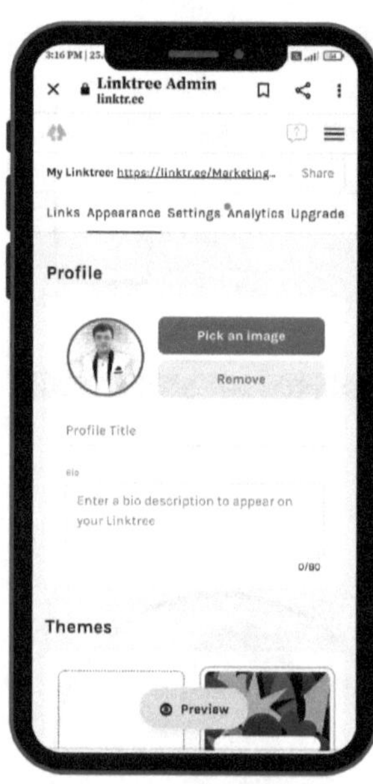

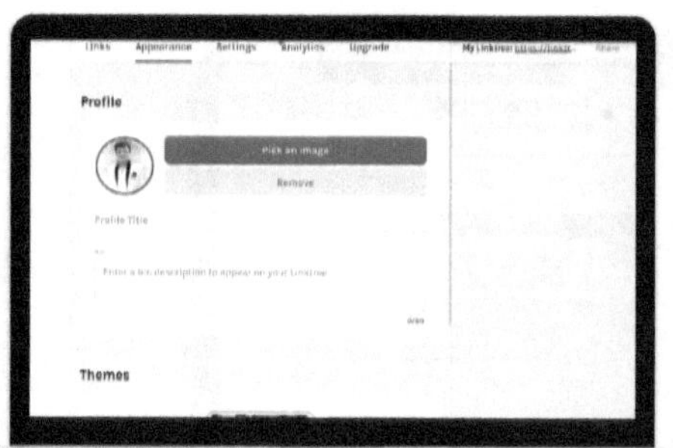

Your landing page will look something like this. You will put the logo of your products. And you can also change the theme of the landing page.

MORE LINKS :

- +91 97111 09725
- WWW.FACEBOOK.COM/MARKETINGHARISH
- WWW.INSTAGRAM.COM/MARKETINGHARISH

• Traffic Source?

There are many free & paid traffic sources for affiliate marketing, where we can sell affiliate products and earn money.

1. Facebook

Facebook is a very good traffic source, because you get here the targeted traffic.

You can grow it by creating your Facebook Groups, Pages on Facebook and when more audience starts coming to your group or page then you can promote your affiliate product.

Similarly, you can promote your affiliate product in other people's Facebook group as well. First of all you have to join the group and give free information to the people there, after that promote your product.

If you follow this strategy for a month, then very soon you will start getting results on Facebook and your products will also start selling soon.

T&C APPLY

MARKETING HARISH

2. Instagram

Nowadays people are using Instagram the most, because the features of Instagram are different and there is a lot of entertainment here, there is a lot of traffic here as compared to the rest of the apps.

To sell affiliate products on Instagram, you have to create an account on Instagram, related to your niche and you will have to post good information on your page. If people like your page, then people will start connecting with you. As soon as your followers increase, then you can earn good money by promoting your affiliate product here.

3. YouTube

Whenever people want some information, people first take the help of YouTube, because here people get good information in less time, YouTube is considered to be the biggest search engine after Google.

Youtube channel also a great platform to earn money. You have to post good videos on your channel daily. To help the logo, and to promote your affiliate product.

You should understand, until you do not have traffic, you will not be able to make money from affiliate marketing, first you have to increase the subscribers on your channel, after that you promote your product.

Q Quora

4. Quora

Quora is a Questions & Answers platform, here you can answer people's questions.

On the Quora website, you get targeted traffic from USA, UK and many other countries. You have to create your account and give information related to your Niche. By writing a review article of your product here, you can publish it here by putting your affiliate link in it.

Medium

5. Medium -

Medium is a very popular article writing platform and this website is mostly used in USA, UK. In these countries, many Affiliate Marketers write articles on this website and also get very good commission from it.

You can write articles by creating your account on the Medium website, if you work here with Consistency, then you can get a sure result here.

• Paid Traffic Source –

• **GOOGLE ADS (ADWORDS)** — you can create an account and pay to display your ads on the top of the search results list, so if a user enters a keyword related to your website, Google will suggest your website.

• **AD EXCHANGE PLATFORMS** — you can sign up to an ad exchange platform, such as Zeropark, and display your ads in the form of pop-ups, banners, push notifications, or native ads (which are ads 'pretending' to be a part of a website).

• **SOCIAL MEDIA ADVERTISING**— you can pay to display your ads on platforms such as Instagram, Facebook (via Facebook Ads Manager), or TikTok so that when a user clicks on your ad they will be redirected to your website/landing page.

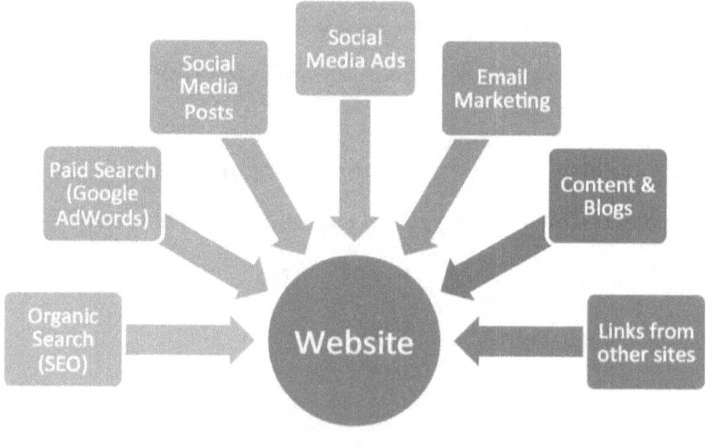

T&C APPLY

MARKETING HARISH

- ## Affiliate Network –

Here I am introducing you some Affiliate Networks, where you can earn a lot.

1. HostGator India - Web Hosting Affiliate Program

Hostgator is one of the top 10 best hosting company in the whole world.

Hostgator gives good service as well as the cheapest hosting.

Hostgator is good and popular affiliate program. If you have good traffic, then you can earn a lot from this: Sale on Hostgator gives you 1250 to 3000 rupees commission and you can earn a lot of money from this.

These 2 types of affiliate programs provide you

Globally affiliate program/www.hostgator.com

Country affiliate program/www.hostgator.in

- # What is Hostgator affiliate eligibility criteria?

You must have a website. Complete SEO will have to be done in the website. While creating the hostgator account, all the complete information will have to be filled completely.

(Note: If interested to buy Domain + Hosting (Just Rs. 79/- per month), just click the link-

https://hostgator-india.sjv.io/2mVRM)

T&C APPLY

• How to Promote Hostgator Affiliate Program?

You can share hostgator advertisement with blog website in any other place, if you want to promote hostgator you can do in these places twitter email marketing, facebook page or all social media to promote. Some affiliate programs do not allow any inappropriate link to be inserted.

2. Bigrock Web Hosting Affiliate Program -

Bigrock affiliate is a very good option for Online Earning through Affiliate Marketing. The best thing about Bigrock Affiliate Marketing Program is that You can share different ads of all these products on your blog and promote them through your blog.

• How to Login Bigrock affiliate ?

If you want to join bigrock affiliate program then it is important for you to have an email from which you can login to bigrock affiliate program because when you sign up bigrock affiliate, it will send bigrock affiliate link to your mail id in which your login id and password will come. Open the email of bigrock affiliate program and log in by entering your email id and password and now you will have to fill the details mentioned here.

User Name - In this box, you have to fill your email, you enter the same email that you use because BigRock Affiliate Program sends link on this mail id and it contains your id and password.

First Name - Now in this you enter your name like if your name is Ashish Jhajhriya, then you have to put only Ashish in it.

Last Name - In this you enter your surname like Ashish Jhajhariya, then put Jhajhriya in it.

Additional Information Company Name - In this you have to enter the name of your company or enter the name of your website.

Address – In this you have to enter your home or office address and keep in mind that you will also have to enter the house number and nearby landmark.

City - In this you have to enter your city meaning city name and keep it in mind, write it correctly.

State - Here you have to enter your state like Uttar Pradesh, Delhi or Haryana, whatever it is

Country - In this you have to enter the name of your country like United States or India or else you have to enter the name of the country in which you live.

Zip code - In this you have to enter the pin code of your area, if you do not know the pin code then you can do a Google search.

Phone no – In this you have to enter your mobile number, the same number that you use

Fax Number - In this you will need to enter your fax number, if you do not have it you can leave it blank

Your Website - In this you open your website and copy and paste its URL

Profession - In this you can enter your profession, you can enter whatever work you do.

Notes: After filling all these details, you read the term and condition given by bigrock affiliate marketing program and then click on I agree term and condition and by clicking on sign up your account will be created.

3. Go Daddy Web Hosting Affiliate Program -

GoDaddy is a very popular brand in the domain name and web-hosting market. They are famous for many reasons and their high-paying affiliate program has all the features that attract any affiliate marketer. The great thing about GoDaddy is that they offer great deals from time to time. Keep coming together, so that you can increase your sales significantly. It is very popular, it is very easy to use it. It is a very trusted brand.

T&C APPLY

• How to join GoDaddy Affiliate Program and start earning money ?

GoDaddy is a very popular in famous for many reasons and their high-paying affiliate program has all the features, that attract any affiliate marketer. I will tell you that before GoDaddy used to have its own managed affiliate program. Later he shutdown his managed affiliate program and started managing his affiliate program through Commission Junction and Viglink. You can join the GoDaddy affiliate program on any of the given marketplaces.

To join Godaddy affiliate program, you have to first come to the godaddy affiliate program page, when you reach the godaddy affiliate page, then you will see the option of join, click on it, then this page will open in front of you. Now fill in the detail you see and submit it, your Godaddy affiliate program will start and from there you can take the link and put it on your site and you can also put godaddy's banner, whichever visitor will come to your site. If he clicks and buys, then you get a very good commission and this is the most trusted site.

T&C APPLY

4. ClickBank -

ClickBank is another affiliate network that has a lot of digital products, though it also offers physical products as well.

You'll find a lot of merchants, who are selling eBooks, online courses, or membership sites. These merchants might not have the name recognition of a national or international brand, but they can be great offers if they fit your niche.

A downbreak with clickbank i.e. some of the ClickBank products just aren't very high-quality products.

And while ClickBank has gotten better with its review process to filter out the bad merchants, you'll still want to be careful about which merchants you choose to promote.

• You have to know about ClickBank -

NICHE/PRODUCT types: ClickBank definitely leans towards digital products, but you'll find some physical products as well (and ClickBank makes it easy to filter between the two).

AVERAGE COMMISSION RATE: Depends on the specific merchant you sign up with, but usually pretty high. You'll find both percentage and flat-rate commissions.

COOKIE DURATION: Depends on the specific merchant you sign up with, but usually ~60 days.

MINIMUM PAYOUT: $10

CLICKBANK®
AFFILIATE PROGRAM

T&C APPLY

48

5. ShareASale -

ShareASale affiliate programs for 4,500+ merchants.

ShareASale is a great option for both digital and physical products.

On the digital side, you'll find a lot WordPress theme and plugin shops, hosting providers, etc.

And on the physical side, you'll find so many big and small merchants.

Basically – no matter what niche your website or blog is in, you can probably find some offers worth promoting.

• Facts about ShareASale -

- Niche/product types: Both physical and digital products.
- Average commission rate: Depends on the specific merchant you sign up with.
- Cookie duration: Depends on the specific merchant you sign up with.
- Minimum payout: $50

6. CJ Affiliate (Commission Junction) -

Commission Junction is one of the TOP 10 affiliate network have about 2500+ different merchants.

Some of the big physical and digital companies using CJ are:

- Lowes
- Overstock
- Office Depot
- Priceline
- GoPro
- IHG (Hotels)
- Grammarly

• About CJ -

- **Niche/product types:** CJ covers a range of niches both physical and digital products.
- **Average commission rate:** Depends on the specific merchant you sign up with.
- **Minimum payout:** $50 for direct deposit or $100 for check.

T&C APPLY

7. Amazon Associates -

If you want to promote physical products on your website, Amazon Associates is a good option.

You can earn a pretty commission at Amazon.com.

• About Amazon Associates -

- Niche/product types: Anything sold on Amazon's website (including products from third-party vendors).

- Average commission rate: Ranges from 1% to 10% depends upon products.

- Minimum payout: $10 for Amazon gift card or direct deposit.

MORE LINKS :

🔘 +91 97111 09725

📘 WWW.FACEBOOK.COM/MARKETINGHARISH

📷 WWW.INSTAGRAM.COM/MARKETINGHARISH

T&C APPLY

BY - HARISH ARORA
(MARKETING & BUSINESS COACH)

WWW.MARKETINGHARISH.COM

TASK 1

Answer the Questions –

1. Are You a DREAMER or ACTION TAKER?

2. What you understand about Lead Magnet?

3. Which kind of Product you Promote according to your niche?

4. Will you like to recommend your known for joining the Affiliate Marketing Course?

TASK 2

Make a Video to describe which kind of strategy you will use in Affiliate Marketing and Upload the same on your any of Social Media Platform with Hashtag #marketingharish .

MORE LINKS :

+91 97111 09725

WWW.FACEBOOK.COM/MARKETINGHARISH

WWW.INSTAGRAM.COM/MARKETINGHARISH

T&C APPLY

BY - HARISH ARORA
(MARKETING & BUSINESS COACH)

WWW.MARKETINGHARISH.COM

• THREE •
DAYS COURSE

PRICE
₹ 9000/-

FREE

hello, Everyone...
how was the course ? I hope you read carefully & seriously. If you want know more about marketing & business call & dm me soon.
thanks.

BY - HARISH ARORA
(MARKETING & BUSINESS COACH)

MORE LINKS :

+91 97111 09725

WWW.FACEBOOK.COM/MARKETINGHARISH

WWW.INSTAGRAM.COM/MARKETINGHARISH

T&C APPLY